CONSOLATION AND MIRTH

ISH KLEIN

CANARIUM BOOKS
ANN ARBOR, MARFA, IOWA CITY

SPONSORED BY
THE HELEN ZELL WRITERS' PROGRAM
AT THE UNIVERSITY OF MICHIGAN

CONSOLATION AND MIRTH

Canarium Books
Ann Arbor, Marfa, Iowa City
www.canarium.org

The editors gratefully acknowledge the
Helen Zell Writers' Program at the University of Michigan
for editorial assistance and generous support.

Cover:
Stills from *The Goat*
Directed by Buster Keaton
Cinematography by Elgin Lessley

First Edition

Printed in the United States of America

ISBN 13: 978-0-9849471-9-5

for Greg C. Purcell

CONTENTS

Gewritu secgað   þæt seo wiht sy
mid moncynne   miclum ticlum
sweotol ⁊ gesyne

from *The Exeter Book*

CONSOLATION AND MIRTH

THIS IS ALSO A DOLPHIN

I do not pay someone
to listen to my problems
because I'm in a progressive
state where therapists are everywhere
and free to the needy.
I'm in the library across
from an office of therapy.
I am watching the hand
in the office window. Clearly,
the hand is the client.
Shit, as soon as I
mentioned it, he retracted it.
Maybe not, yeah, it's back.

There's a ring on him.
He pretends to be whisking
an egg. Now bouncing atop
the blond armrest. He opens,
lifts as if listening to
music; or he is palsied.
Period. It's away now. Period.
No! It's back doing *capisce*;
understand in Italian. Lily bud.
It is a pale hand. He's
pointing now. Fist hitting his
armrest. He's opened fingers, it's
away from the window. No,

it's back. It's up near

his chest then hits armrest.
Maybe this is a woman?
Now it's whisking in tighter
circles, presumably, a smaller egg.
Less work, less concern. Why
did I assume masculine previously?
It was a thick ring.
But women do that too:
wear thick rings. It's 50/50.
The hand was not hairy.
Our hands are bigger now.
It's gone. Now it's back

up: bouncing. Nervous but insistent
Who knows what this hand
does away from the window?
In the sticky ear, poking
its owners nose. Pointing. It's
pointing. Rude or raw confidence.
Now it's two hands pointing.
Hello! It's like a chevron.
Bouncing, now the sign for
money: fingers wearing each other
out. It's away from its
window. I'll give it five
minutes. I don't have forever.

It's back at a new
angle. I see the polar

fleece sleeve of the owner.
which blends with the reflection.
Yes, it's back; arched like
a sea creature. Now out
of the window, now bobbing
over the armrest energetically.
He or she is dealing
with agitation. He or she
is not touching down now.
The hand unfurls; less weapon,
more emphasis. It diffusely points.

It points over there, beyond
the still life on the wall.
Now the "eh" sign, *comme
si, comme ça*. Slowing down.
Maybe he or she got
sedation. A headless body towards
me. Hello, Therapist! Nice shirt.
He lumbers with a pad.
The hand leaves the room.
Out for more problems, probably.
No, I reframe that story.
Now, she is reaching out.
Now, they come towards her.

TACTILE ALPHABET

(A)   Left hand touches the right shoulder.
Hand holds the shoulder
Varying placement and strength of grasp.

(B)   Right hand touches the left shoulder.
Note differences if differences exist.
Replicate activity, note changes in brain wave,
head pressure or jaw tension level.

(C)   Hand over but not touching skin. Maybe you are
covered with subtle hair on your skin.
Some hair may be coarse. Scars are hairless.

(D)   A body that belongs to you. When in debt,
do not.

(E-G)   Image – Snow on volcano. Transpose
onto this an image of a barnacle-like size.

(F)   That the "f" phase drops out,
many people schedule a vacation
or take a break. They leave for one day.

There is a crater on the moon. I hope to obtain
an image of this. I intend to size it right
along with the volcano and the barnacle and light

the three together. Note, range and time.
Weather on the moon still a question.

(H)   Whether here, the "H" enters the Great phase
        Witness the birth of the word "ghreat":
        it means: very good before and now and different.

(I)   Lowercase and dotted
        as with helmet. Me before I knew you:
        dreaming volcano.

(K})   Phase of misspelled claims.

(L}})   Low time.

(M}})   Someone different goes into debt now.

(N})   A mean professor gathered into care.

(O)   Ode for a lobe.
        That is ode you.

(P)   Then personally to give the images that had gone Missing.

(Q)   Questions from the fifties: Cybervibe history.

(R)   Rest. Stop.

(S)   S'up.

(T)   Tiles.

(U)   Under-equals

(V)   A sight of hand is Victory.

(W)   When the last four become a butterfly —

(X)   It cannot be typed by you may draw it by hand with
        chalk on a wall.
        The "X" signature in the center.

(Y)   Add over this "Y" to face the earth, then one "Y" to face
        the sky.

(Z)   Then 90 degrees clockwise "z" atop the 180 degrees "z".

        Try to draw it if you like

            the lines are simple

                and they work together

                    definitely willing to fly.

INVERSE HEAVEN DIVISION TWO

The family was uncertain — wind with sand,
within the staid breath, shuddering

a flame flares then falls like a shield before a cup of spirits.
A complex comes up to a desert; a fine c.

Add water from an amphora.
Someone summoned as by ship. Division Two

up for the ashes. The ashes had their time
by the flame. I cannot speak of pure carbon

only what is bound here to be burned again. A cup
of spirits convinces one to sell their dearest treasure

for sight then for gold then for wine then for more time.
What fox, this soul thief, shifting fur

and see the dough creep.
Guile in a hard landscape.

What family remains composed the jar,
a Lot. A cock with hens. A Lot.

If the father is uncertain,
possibly cuckoo, do you

blame the daughter who turned into water
to summon a ship?

Separation: takes these creatures from their storage,
takes these girls from being creatures.

There is no one who can say, you are mine.
For me you were made.

He turns into a millstone who says that is so.
He loses his treasure, his anchor and his soul.

EGGHEADS AND REJECTS IN AND AROUND SCIENCE FICTION SOCIETY

And of course when I say 'reject' it is meant
as self-reject. There is only the self, empty,
no inherent meaning but for flow.

I have been in the hall where certain people
have not succumbed to television. So I tell you:
grateful I am that you can be not so scrambled

and with memory. I have undergone the reject
stamp, somewhere in the back of my head
my soul said yes to the scientists, yes to the scab.

I think it was a capture in a game
like isolated pawn.
No I do not like isolated pawn.

Rejects, please meet up with me on disc 4.
Rejects, please realize that we have to go slow.
On four we talk about the beautiful things of our time.

I will start: I loved the thought of Christmas:
lights and color. Cold very cold, only horses.
It is remote. I give them the square cigar boxed scene:

animals in outfits dance on mirrored glass.
Handiwork A++, the sky, diamonds in the glint,
geometry, little bit of moss, going slow, etc..

I will make them proud; maybe even frighten them
with my big magnifying-lens head.
They will give me a coat to go with the rest of my life.

In the wings are the joke shows.
The ongoing notes.
The fret of nothing.

I heard tell about the horrible pink foam, for instance:
save us from the foam; the foam as fixative holding up the boat.
I've heard how the upper level is dreck

and therefore we are below dreck, we feeble people.
I tell myself I must not believe this honky speech.
Then dream, the shaved head with scab in the sun,

then someone took a picture.
How horrified was I?
Over 50% then I went to bed.

The flea of a machine, conceive.
The circus I run to;
an organized show of things practiced.

I will blow out a canon, then come back.
Every little leaf of my skin
right back intact, my fly trick or trap.

There are many now who will shrewdly
be waiting with their cameras,
I'm not happy to say.

Though I've fixed its hold on me.
I've fixed it so they will not see.
"They" are the guards apart who love only their own trained dogs.

Eggheads who have determined.
Eggheads who cannot conceive.
Eggheads who are from somewhere cleaner.

Why not get a pawn turned queen in here?
You from quiet prosperity
do not get the thickness of our skin

nor its astounding capacity for callous
nor its borted capillariel cones
nor its consequence-bisect hearts.

You who grew up around a soul
whereas we are coral
underwater, we build ground up

from almost nothing
which is what we love.
A ride to the movies, the ride home from the movies

P.A.F.S. NEWS

PHILADELPHIA ALTERNATE SCIENCE FICTION SOCIETY

JANUARY NEWSLETTER

Acknowledged, I am not the usual newsletter writer in the group.
I've taken over, the Weinbergs will be fine; the list was public.
I have a name; I'm at meetings;
I volunteer: two hours table work at PHILCON.
Optimal weight and gloss of palm card was my thing.

VALUE! I mentioned the gem of the navel and the gold rope.
PLUS I help subtly with stories. (PERCEIVE: I will not abuse
the slash and dot: !) The Philadelphia Science Fiction Society
should know me well enough. The others.
They have been vocal on air while I appeal to your mind: print.

Our next meeting January 29, speaker TBA.
(Probably someone from the computer. Probably Sleet Field,
the video game maker and, face it, toy salesman.)
Pamphlets? No, no. Location: the Weinbergs':
3207 Rawlings St. Philadelphia at 7:30 pm.

Rory Feldstein and his stories that are dummy thugs!
That wasn't in the minutes: Monopolist.
Great Feldstein; our god Feldstein. What?
To be in the minutes, in the clique all the way, right.
Timing for idiots. Time!

Alternates, have you noticed that in your minutes
you only detail the minutes of the previous meeting?
And those minutes were an account of the minutes
of the last month's meeting?!
Can you not get past this? Can you not progress?

And your table at PHILCON was unsuccessful because
none of you know KUNG FU of the real. In plain sight
with your action figures. Forever fingering. The backstabbing
pea-brained sadists at the Philadelphia Science Fiction Society
may be illegal but they know how to work a table.

They know how to show up near the windmills where Harlan
Ellison weeps. They've got information; they slay and play
with it while you are all in the grey; okay occasional black.
That you are nicer to Feldstein. Nicer won't get you anywhere!
Your cares and contaminations? (Who cares about your cats?)

I assume like most sci fi initiates you are going for the gold
metaphor, the key. I can contribute. Octavia Butler was worried,
way back, I was so on the scene. I was so everywhere. I said,
"I'm Abraham!" "Oh irony" said she mentally. "No, the Lincoln
 bust in the movie. Angela Isselin kissing the son with tongue."

(The first movie based on the book.
Manchu Can Can Consciousness.
FUNG KU.)
I laid tracks for the railroad when I first got here.
Now this music. Jazz.

Ocatavia was just about to read. Why don't our special guests read?
Can they not read the scene? Are they only meant to gawk
and hawk plastic figures or layered mazes their minds line up
to the motherboard. Bed fed, digital light. Oh one, oh one.

We say alternate; well, let's prove it.
New minutes, for instance.
New guests of the mineral given due respect.
Why do you not believe a practiced alternate
can handcraft faster than mimeograph?

This is why PHILCON was crap.
It wasn't the economy.
Who among you has ever had a job?
Laying tracks for instance?

I assumed you are sci fi because of truth imperative
instead it's just coffee shop after the minutes loop.
At coffee all the talk is about Harlan Ellison's round bed.
I've pissed on Harlan Ellison's round bed!

Not to be paperback
but on stone.
Base for the bust or break.
Come Beethoven, old big head,
the cock, the pen of God

god. G- ggg gggit seems believe,
I, O and N end. The Funk in the breast.
Alternates! Alternates!
Will we ever even once meet up?
With me, I mean?

FROM A BOOK OF CHANGES

I was looking for the book of me to throw
at the book of you and this is what I found:
It's one book. Not exactly square;

at times yes, 90° angles. You pull a page up what ho!
like a bed sheet and underneath is you and me and something
like a dragon boat. It begins in the mouth.

The first page is dirt you put dirt in your mouth
and spit it out. We read trails and pulls and weezes.
I put palm leafs on our heads and call us sage pages.

You say, now chocolate.
I say stomachache. You say no fun.
I say you are too white, you say no way

and work at the edge to pull a sheet off this argument. Look!
A drunk is asleep. You think help him. I say he's bleeding acid
call the family, you say the family's the problem,

I say so what? they have to and you say k(no)w they don't.
You wake the drunk and he yells you are trying to kill him.
You say get the F—— out of my book.

He says it's his book whitey; you direct him to me and say whitey-er.
I say I am albino and therefore blacker than both your sorry asses
in terms of non-standard. I go to prove it in the book

and the drunk starts eating the book.
You put your hand in his mouth, I put my hand in his nose,
doing this we three become dogs, the book becomes a glowing hand,

its little finger in the drunk dog's mouth.
The drunk dog says F—!, the hand leaps from his mouth and clamps
onto my throat, the drunk dog bites my scalp.

I scream and you run around us in circles yapping.
The drunk dog starts lowering me into the ground
then the hand grips the drunk dogs tail, twisting it.

They whirl around and you slow your yap run.
I bleed and my blood becomes a red plastic bucket.
You start to mention my plastic blood and I say F—

into your brain. We watch the drunk dog with the hand
on his tail while backing up.
I say you should talk to the hand

and you laugh into my brain. I say seriously.
You say the drunk dog had it coming.
You become a general; I am private first class.

I decide to put the hand into the bucket somehow.
The bucket's handle tastes like a Mexican worm bar snack.
I say this into your brain. You say la di da.

You move to the right so that I must follow with my mind.
I turn and the drunk dog is asleep, the hand is nowhere visible.
I say the hand! The hand! My bucket becomes a red vinyl collar

you say you will wear it!
I say, the hand! You say you will wear the collar.
I do not know how to say no. I worry.

I might need it. You put it together in your mind.
You leave. I reconsider the collar. You leave. And the hand!
I start howling like a cartoon coyote.

You will send letters, grit in my eyes from South America.
I say would they like me in a blimp, General?
You say a blimp? Is your name on it, private?

I become tired. I decide to call the drunk dog's family
by bloody bandages on their clotheslines
and spitting DNA all over the place.

They come and they see what has happened: his being a dog.
They are nice to him. I say he will change probably soon
anyway it isn't bad being a dog and I realize he is leaving

and I realize he is leaving and I realize
I become pollen in your eyes.
I say inside your brain I hate you instant whole

and you laugh inside my brain and say I am a hole
and you are a whole and I say no way General
and you say you are so a whole, private.

SPECIAL

I read that to say you are "special" is to mistake
your condition. It is a reason people remain paranoid,
      the notion of chosen.

In spite of this I beheld a special's notion.
      Virginia from church.
A situation: *Isaiah* (called forth)   textbook of specialness.

That she had taken the chalice I saw;
I saw that she gave it to me to drink.   I let it.
      I drank to my sister's disgust.

Left unattended. I remember laughing. A kind
of understanding was between us.   A person
controls a person.   Is that not special?

Anyway, Virginia and Maria.
They were in Church every Saturday
at 5 p.m. just like me and the others.

Later I saw Virginia without Maria;
      and bought a drawing from her on Park Ave.
called 'Lady of Spain.'

One could definitely see a lady
and Spain a flower
      on her head of variable red.

ON A LEVEL

IN THIS LEVEL FEAR IS THE MEDIUM
IN THIS WAY I AM A TRUE STOMACH

WHAT COMES INTO THE MOUTH GOES THROUGH ME
AND EXITS OR BECOMES STRUCTURAL

IN EITHER CASE IT GOES AWAY
IN EITHER CASE I REMAIN HERE

I DO NOT KNOW THE FUTURE AT ALL
I DO NOT KNOW THE STRUCTURE VERY WELL

SOME STOMACHS BECOME TOO FULL OF MUCUS
A WIDE TUBE OF CRAMPS AND UNDRY GLUE

THEY STARVE THEIR ORGANISM SLOWLY
AND THEY TOO DIE OR ARE HELPED BY MEDS

SOME SAY THEIR COURSE WAS SELF DESTRUCTIVE
THOUGH MAYBE IT IS NATURAL TO MOVE

I AM AMBIVALENT AS STOMACH I FEAR MEDS
I KNOW THE MAN WHO LIVES IN THE BRAIN

I DO NOT WANT TO STARVE HIM
I STAY AWAY FROM THE MAN WHO LIVES IN THE BRAIN

STOMACHS AND BRAINS MUST NOT TOUCH IT MUST
BE LEARNED OR THE STOMACH RISKS FILLING

OUR HUMAN HOST WITH BRAIN DESTROYING ACID
WHICH WILL ALSO CAUSE HIM MOUTH AND JOINT PAIN

OR HIS BRAIN WILL EJECT ME NATURALLY
WITH THE MUCUS GHOSTS

AND I WILL BE A BLADDER OF MUCUS
IN AN ANIMAL FREE LANDSCAPE

THEORETICALLY I AM ALREADY THERE
I MENTION TO THE BRAIN I MAY BE DONE

WITH CIRCULATION I WILL MOVE OUT SCREW FEAR
HE SAYS MY ENVIRONMENT IS ALWAYS ME

GHOSTS EVERYWHERE I GO HE SAYS I WOULD FEEL
AFRAID AND SWAMPED WITH MATERIAL

I AM TREATED TO PICTURES OF STILLBORNS
AT THIS STAGE I WOULD BE A STILLBORN

I AM SWAMPED IN THE ACID OF THE BRAIN
WHICH KEEPS THE ORGANS IN THEIR PLACE

WHICH IS IMPORTANT TO THE HUMAN
AND THE PRECIOUS HUMAN FAMILY

THE MAN IN THE BRAIN HAS HIS OWN STOMACH
EVERYONE IN HIS FAMILY DOES

I AM JUST AN ENVIRONMENTAL INDICATOR
WELCOME TO THE NEW FULL EMPLOYMENT

HE SAYS TO STOP COMPLAINING
YOU ARE LUCKY TO BE ANYWHERE

I AM LUCKY TO HAVE THIS WORK
WORK WORK WORK WORK RWOK OWRK WR0K KROW O

O IS A HUG   K IS A PUNCH IN THE FACE
W IS SHAME   R IS A ROSE

A BOOK DESCRIBES MY COMMON PROBLEMS
A STRUCTURAL INCOMPLETENESS

A RESULT OF OPIATES MILK AND WHEAT
WHILE FORMING WITH FEAR

LOOKING BEYOND MY SPECIALIZED FLESH
I WAS WARNED BY THE LUNGS AGAINST THIS

BRAIN FLASH JUDGE NOT LEST YE BE JUDGE
I UNDERSTAND BRAIN THAT I DO NOT UNDERSTAND

WHILE FORMING MEANING
YOU WERE HOMELESS HE SAID

YOU FELL PREY TO A MIRACULOUS
INJECTION WHICH GAVE

THE ABILITY TO RELAX ESCAPE ETC
YOU ARE HOOKED ON THE ESCAPE THING

THAT IT COULD BE OUT THERE WAS AMAZING
BUT IT WAS A BITCH TO SECURE

YOU THINK YOU ARE GETTING ONE THING
IT TURNS OUT TO BE A VIRUS

SO THAT IS WHAT IT WAS
I AM SORRY FOR WHOEVER MAY HAVE TAKEN UP

THAT CRAVING   YOU CAN LET GO
OLD PEOPLE TELL ME THAT FEAR IS AN ILLUSION

THIS IS WRONG FEAR IS FIRST WATER
FROM THERE YOU MOVE ON

TO THE HIGH WIRE OR THE TRAPEZE
AS A GOOD IDEA

                              OR FROM THE LUNGS AS AIR

I THOUGHT THIS WAS A COLD HOUSE

Is she a father splinter:
one who comes to every class
as a face on a poster
or more so a carrier
who sidles like sidlers do?

If someone called me that name
I'd invert with some outrage.
I am not your mother-boy.
What is this, then? Being Made.
What is this, then? Compulsions.

Everywhere are everywhere
things. Images of eyes are
eyes and we just don't settle.
We go after her cold house.
Why do we hate old women?

You open an old woman
and there are at least ten kids
and one hundred old men-types
holding tens of tens of kids
while their bodies slowly grow.

I don't care like them kids there.
Song be: This Is New Today
this new old man, a new boy,
a new boy/girl and woman.
You, you, you. You new, you new.

LIKE ON THE SUBJECT OF THE ICEBREAK

I mean <u>light</u> on the subject of the icebreak
please do not think this is bad wording
because of the incorrect word above me right now in
the title I have even closer to me now provided.

(Letter Machines! – Just don't. Don't. Could you not?)

Here the talking. The sharp end of sentence.
It cuts a reasonable voice down
in spite of the unreasonable intersection.

Correct word: <u>light</u>/ which I underline and to the side
for you to see and it is a bonus I will underline
all the <u>lights</u> for you to see, for you see we must,
by what I'm trying to manage –

THE ICEBREAK/ how is meant the prevalent
icebreak which are a true and natural threat.
For there is danger in the ghoats mountains.
The ghoat mountain falling from the sky.

Now, BEHOLD A BEING BOUND TO MOUNTAIN, neither
   goat nor ghost.
Little Ms. Jones – a very pretty host.
Did she think this world of woe was a world of woe?
Actually no and that did not unbound her.

Where is she, exactly? In the ice
inside the Mountain, Silly.

A hospital bed, in this poem.
A very rudimentary hospital,
with a wire encircling her head
to zap the over-persuading lice.

Do you hear me, Ms. Jones?! I'm calling help —
Do not breathe the carbon monoxide, breathe only the mostly
  beige
oxygen mix. PLEASE! Do not worry about your contact lens
or any other meniscuses in your head.

I am gathering to save you!

do you think my friend
the example is a conjuring trick?
Do you think she is *playing* dead?

Well, yes, you are right she is and fine
too truly dead only apparently/ fine tuned dread indeed.
Mrs. Jones, her mother my dear friend,
you see and little Ms. Jones her scion.

So you get me. We had a thing — the mother and me
a magic act. I should have made it only a minute.
I should not have allowed
DO NOT SAW A WOMAN IN HALF WITHOUT THE BOX

no matter what the other one wants.
What I mean as you see — I am an experienced man

and I see that we are all mostly men
having left in mountains our girls. Here men

pump letters; looking for approval or hair raising
What is the most in secret. What is the Most.
Let me see right down my own big open mouth
to the logical conclusion if this is no occlusion

Stomach what do you say
that I can translate?
Maybe cell walls of the vegetable.
We need four walls for the stanza, three to be free.

Which cell am I breaking out of, you may wish to know?
which cell! As of off a tree? Exactly
very good. *Is it stomate let us say?*
My friend STOW MATE My friend

We briefly break out in three
that's the spirit
broken through a wall!

Simultaneously you. I risk
obnoxiousness in saying instead of naming
you with the space in your name – you are
awakening, I notice. It burns by turns and shakes.

Your own Ms. Jones: Yourself in the small eye reflection.
Someone looks up to you, look under the lid.

Angry bears 'til I figure it out.
Angry homelessness is bears, I fear.

You who may be just around the corner
you have just purchased a twelve-pack
and are at once happy and too disturbed
at how fast you drank that last twelve pack.

You tell yourself you aren't but you are and that is natural.

And with this twelve-pack you will sit before
advertisation light that will simulate investment
in a fate of winning a game and you will
become excited later.

Very excited
because it means to you: recognition of excellence
invisible mountaineers would soon put straight
You, You, You! with the beer.

All 780,000 of you.
But I am only talking to you with the space!
Maybe you can hear me I am
high pitched calling to you initiate!

The secret Ms. Jones to break out
and your own cold people from the Invisible M-T-N?
Who indeed could hold a line so close
and carefully as to bring back to one's own bosom

the frames and vocabularies of our ancestors
for the challenging now architecture!
Who? Me!
and You with the space.

And when the more Reals wake up to slap and paste and smooth
our holey brains we will say thank you with resentment, I fear.
They will have the advantage of handicraft which we will fear
but we will be careful not to show our fear.

To deal with their disdain we will make a holiday.
For 90 seconds we will fill the air
with our sulfurous gossip about these ancestors, the air will burn
like personnel firework. The clichéd independence day.

Had you been pale before this,
and you know you were Mrs. Jones,
you will finally be tan.
Your daughter piebald and loving it!

You — ocean of beer, seer!
you will have rhythms astounding.
And someone who is not you.
A lady or a tiger.

Old Children will run around in wheels
The ash from the sky will breed new plants.
The plants will want to strangle us at first
Light remember this was to crest

above a point; above time.
An adjustment. And comeback.
And now we know the snow has been falling.
We call what falls snow and it falls

on clichéd cemeteries and people on their birthdays.

There are others who are better at meeting the beings

the snow has not yet touched and touching them.

They are not so likely to get mixed up personally.

They were us once.

BOWS FROM THE LAST DANCE

Not enough left to make sure a swan stays
a swan until the end of the last act.

New strings need new arrangements, better bows,
a whole evening   you weren't dreaming.

A progression of swan to court lady
requires a peasant girl in between.

Calculator, to me these things you show:

    a calculator act requires a show

not a new lady dreaming between stays.

SCIENCE FICTION SOCIETY

EACH OF THESE RIDDLES HAS A SOLUTION

R O

I   a   word
births me.
          Who on earth
am I?
                    Or what on
earth is
                    not the word
 I am?
                    Inverse the
woe or man
                    tell the man,
what now?
          .

R 1

Before our life, there was life though no
light pooled there. A stranger-taking
life makes less light. Know me Stranger
and then shed your interior
death. Now, who do you think I am?

R 9

Who was it who told
you that you must have
been totally in
sleep? Opening
the light of seconds?

R 2

One without me may look
upon a brilliant day
but may not wheel towards
or away. Say my name
to start to know me now.

R i

Thirst is father to the storm.
Fire bell until alarm.
Millstone becomes uncertain.

Drawing on face, a spirit
mainly takes. Small animals
break. Who do they say I am?

R 24

If in thought there is
often no control,
fire can find me
see what weights the air.
Say what you see there.

R 17

He reached out to   you.
You took this,   it   was
       accurate   language
to see you through   death.
Why do you   say death?

R 8

Before you move your hand to move
before the thought to do is me.
Can you say and stare this one down?

R 13

I am not moving.
I told you so. I
told you I was cold.
And only just me.
Dare to say my name.

R 20

Here goes a page now,
now an owner. Say
who can hear a twig
speak while on the tree?
Say who she is now.

R 7

Towards fire worlds move
not a battery
rather a stored hand
opening our ice
and seed. What is it?

R 6

Two are stamping feet
on my roof ceiling.
Men and women meet
to see me outdoors.
State my name plainly.

R 19

As a greenery
you would grow most here.
Conditions being
dear. Some protection.
Of what do I speak?

R 12

A gene is not this
nor is a collar
surprising like this.
I'm for your pleasure.
Say what you think I am.

R 16

His head is an instant
that looks like lightning.
A trace taken form. Your
wild life in our woods.
Who are you like this?

R 15

From where you begin
the grass gets held down.
Holding then sailing –
the will and motion.
What's all this about?

R 10

Will I walk towards this?
Give it all of me?
An animal not
an animal. What's
happening to me?

R iv

My name is No One.
I own this building
and half of your town.
I sold the other
half to your rival.
I buy high and sell
higher. I will get
your seed bank. I am
fun. Say what I mean.

R 23

Below light it finds
turf and turns it up.
Lines indicate time
physical and strength
giving. Guess my name.

R 21

The thought of you made
new words for new men
and women. Your cloak
protects early words.
How are you these days?

R 22

It's happy, it wants
to arrive. It makes
to arrive. At this
we say 'happy.' It's what?

MEDITATIONS IN A LIGHTING EMERGENCY

"Look, you shouldn't look when someone tells you to look."
This sac on the head
"My," "I" meaning ours
like the bear.
Lights the song.
Losing faces in the bag—
Night.
In here is ink:
bugs and commitment.
Creepy it hears thought.
Presence in general peaks.
Ring lit speech's missing protections—
Not the caul it's radiation.
One close to none.
Meaning slight existence.
That I am because of you, for instance.
"In the light upon the ring and in the empty part—"
"May we all be so" no
"May we not be so!"
Your water on my ground!
It is saying it is not a fold.
So don't call me a fold.

MISS IS NOT . . .

My Science says that what were once devils now
are tape worms: big ones! Hence a no pork rule.
And as ever these worms are among us.

Voice altered by an intestinal eye
       Look out, look out, look out, look out, look out
and they want cow milk and nice white sugar.

'Here I have one places to fill: you! you!'
Fight it out dummies, then get back to me.
       CONTRA "we need everything, everyone"

But. It's not at the same rate of exchange.
I am annoyed at you. I'm a baby.
The useful machines that bloomed from my corpse

I do not want to be their food no more.
Can't we negotiate now about this?
Regarding my bedroom of saliva.

I just want to keep it, can I keep it?
'No Miss,' said him from old Romania
with a mouth full of me: damn damn damn damn

'you must be pessimist', 'circumspect', 'strong.'
That's your damage, buddy, not me, you dig?
I am out here too and want to be free.

And in so far as the cave, well, I'll go!
Something like the swiftlet who make nests from
saliva! I will not graduate! Yikes.

What will happen to my life? The gutter?
The gutter snipes or gutter sniping, hmmm.
So fucking what? So dee la fucked-dee woo.

No yan wo edible nest swiftlet noo.
Was this fair to my spirit? It's my spit!
My spit that eventually went toward

the other thing the other thing outside.

CIRCULAR RUNES

It knew it was a fortune and initial —
only itself, for all that came before
was not this fortune.

It tended to become big with baloney
though it would walk often watching
its feet — the fact that it had meat
made of this an ox who drew lines in the earth.

Take to this a hammer. Or if nature made a branch
nearby to a rock and if in the ox's line
it so happens the branch comes across
a rock and if this makes an impression
on the ox — a thorn is born. A hand is born —

And some would say a man is born but he isn't man-like yet.
Taking elements and shaping them together Birthing
is born, the brain is born, he who makes
is born. He finds a branch then finds what made this —
he finds a tree
and builds with this his reach —

A chariot conveys this way.
Before we knew each other but we didn't
know who or what 'who' had to be
necessarily. Moving — yes. He can write,
he can move it from his hand
to your head. He can mark wood
with a word. He can make you see incompletely

and so starts the world burning
incompletely – the outer rags written.
They said to burn them. Torch each word.
This world had six elements
and fragmentation.
There was suspicion – they said, 'kill him'.
He hid in his hat.
His hat began to burn.

And in burning he was lifted,
being above it he was saved.
The body went away,
a gift remained. It moved
under ash like a bump in a landscape.
This gift had him come back
for it was something he could not conceive.
It was a new
being.

And because it could not speak at first
it was joy. A return to pre-word
was the world-joy unapart.
He would hold this to be whole.
He would heat it and feed it
and take to it what of earth
he could find and he would hide
it from beasts when he needed to leave it alone.
Beasts sensed this
and resented it.

Stones of ice fell from the sky.
He with joy cannot hide
from those in need.
He is pursued, he is chased
and forced to reveal his life-gift.
He is frightened for it.
That it should be battered
or become perpetually in need
like those beings who would pull it
to pieces. He fights until exhausted.
His life-gift he buries and land grows over it at a madcap rate.

Enter the ice.
Hiding moving,
hiding time.
So, separated, the life-gift stopped
while he climbed,
he left
many words
to the life-gift.
The year was silent.
DO
NOT
THINK

You will see I have grown smaller than a bead,
though my feet are big as stars and my hair
can fill the universe. As a small drop
of water flows into a tree.

From the ice I have come to moving again
choosing a corridor from the forest floor.
I am drunk by one yew tree.
Thee tree who did not crash
took me
from ice
though by ash sown
the seed
saved like he from the fire.

As by fire they were pured
so by water I am pured.
Knowing holding
having been held.
Knowing going I went
to a memory preserve.
A strange communication
from the north as leaves
seem to return mirth – a consolation.
Happy to have shown you
needed a green spark
to show you
something else grows
inside an earthen bowl.

From the forest comes an elk
and on his branches sky-feeling
and in his eyes
come hunters

and for a fawn
remote instinct
as from need grows some ability.
This will not live indoors
nor be well made
for machines.
You can accept his strength
is more than equal to yours.
You will eat
his flesh after
draining his blood.

Such is what the sun does
coming to the surface.
Blood being the current and course
of your life through time.
Your life comes up
to meet the sun.
You like
rare heat.
A hot spring.
The sun has hidden
too in the center
an energy store.
Only words could make
possible an instant
still place
in the forest.

Above all this
a construction holds the sky
in place. A birch tree
sees to silver – a sense
takes sticks,
puts words there
to burn the words.
The birched word conjured
to be purged.
My life looks at this work
with fear. It can
never really
be part of anything
nor is it ever out of the way.
The name is stated.
He is called to claim me;
to put me in a form further out.

He does not show caring.
I do not show caring.
I act the fire cycle:
In my dream, I fight a horse child
for a prestigious prize while
a large shark eats some of me
unseen. I perceive and see nothing.
Then he comes back. Appearing
on water. A numinous float,
a mail barge, the letter says,
"There's no beating the oven.

You can leave with your one life.
That is, if you will have life.
A basket on a river.
Ice and downhill motion.
Attached, unattached. No one
is permanently frozen."
So my time keeping ends this way.

The
clay
and
indentation
earth
folds
to
a
new
day.
What
can
be
taken
will
be
taken
home
finally.

GOLE 83

Today the sun died at one twenty five.
Chimes in the future in dreams in the future.
It is not beautiful to be alone.
And I am not alone. You are with me.
Good reality is a strength habit.
Our house is good though dies when we leave it.
My name is erased: chalk off the pavement.
But the names you say stand up from the grave.
What good is praise? What good is a name?
My body cycles a place in a way.
It was a job, it is a job. I do
work. This planet equally weighted
by five grave futures names alone do create. Pavement
habit you call it as you lift me away from it.

INVERSE HEAVEN DIVISION ONE

In   verse heaven   division   one
there is no memory,   there   are
water, wheels and   mangrove   trees.

Charges   of   physicality.
One plane positive poised to bond
with negatives who come through by

water. Beginning in   Brookland,
land of love   and vodka   tonic.
Water   with   an   acid   reacts

with the blood. Without water – I
die, without water   the form dies,
with water   forms   may overflow.

It seems to have no form to name.
If I start   human   from   water,
I may act   crazy   or off course

It   is   a   human   doing this.
This poem's form is supposed to be
uhhh   iambic   tetrameter.

Now you know this I can   fill   it
with water as you do drinking jars.
Filling   is   the   singing.   Singing

is   participating.   Water
rises   in my brain with a charge.
Look up! I may be a light brigade.

Why   my   heavens   are   divided
by   my   personal   dilation:
see flowers called morning glory.

A   sphere,   an atom,   a blender.
Pure   water can come from boiling
if you have the proper   glassware.

And I   often wondered   how I
ended up here? What sort of wheels
aligned and deemed it time for me

to experience the times of people?
What cart delivered me from a past
which had no place   for my mind's

future? For my eyes to see clearly
how   not   to   embody   disease.
The   outside out,   the inside in.

People   survive   under   bridges
in packs   with alcohol;   no fixed
place.   People at   home all alone

like me   eating   television.
Who's poorer me or   street people?
Street people,   naturally, I think

I can   go   inside.   I am in,
hidden   from   authority   figures.
Refracted   cases   rule here.

Not   for   me   to   be   a ruler.
I have been   near this;   a near miss.
The wheel moves from running water.

From   rain   I'd say   we're all
just   okay.   The behavior   changes

but the names all blend.   A person
can   change   their   name
and   what   they   say   is   changed.

In   rare   situations   something
begins   to adapt   and then thrive.
From a   new name informing others.

The   red   mangrove   does   this;
it lives in salt water. The author
of me and my name's   electricity.

BRIDGE RHAPSODY

Tir na nÓg   land of perpetual youth
spirals behind my south occipital.
If you are not from here, looking back does not break your neck.

In the view from Cincinnati, I'm in a coma
in a charity ward. My heartbeat is vertical
and tries the horizontal with regularity.

In the view from Old Antarctica,
I am nothing but a battery.

In the view from the concrete in the Brooklyn Bridge
I am a low flying plane that could finally
get them out of there.

Sense impending capture.
My clock face breaks vibrating concrete.
Smoke settles before my face.

I was so late to work that day;
my spirit taken into a bridge.

He stopped his car, his girlfriend nervous.
I asked what happened; you've got a really bad cut, he said

and drove off; thus escaping the counter clock.
The local custom is not to get implicated.

At the hospital, Dr. Football posed before me with a needle.
I asked for plastic surgery. Not possible said he.
Then butterflies.

Butterflies?! Butterflies are exactly the opposite!

The Going mechanism and the Striking mechanism
separate that day.
In the view from Old Germany, I am a mental defective

deported in a bus. In the view from the National
Institute for Health, I am an animal
systematically stressed by varying intensities of electricity.

In the view from Kalamazoo, I am a toppled tree
that bursts forth baby mice.
A convenience store for hoards,

Tir na nÓg   the underwear
the counting wheel. In her teeth, the promise of atomized joy.

Every word you've heard, turns and torques
the desires around me.
Believers in the star witnessors.

Kids harnessed to apocalyptic power sources.
I mind this weight furnishing my motor power.
My chest is what the weight cord wound around.

In my opinion, unwinding the hour wheel is code
blue; therefore useful to move a great wheel.
I move as a second wheel, I escape opinion.
See V – the verge where pallets mesh in the cogs of the escape wheel.

In the view from Rome, I am red shoes.
I balance by Folio, I have some tee. I attach to the top
of the verge and so swing with it.
Weights shift as per adjustment.

In the view from Valley Medical, I am a diagnostic tool.
In the view from the kitchen, I throw out indigestible food.

Note the Striking mechanism coming together,
the projection for Detent,
the Bell hammer. Salt over metal –

That sound is releasing the wheel and pinion.

It is the sound of someone, me in fact

someone of several frequencies

who has taken to escaping systems

who has taken herself into the sea fold

who has taken herself out of this time.

LINE OF REALITY

Fate is just an ocean, right.
Humans left do anything. It seems

like somewhere sleepy. Certainly the bedsheet left a screen
for a start; like putting up your right hand

to make right a rabbit heart or a lying man.
Shadows before every left thing are huge.

And dark folds, a material left to hide inside, to become bold.
My time as pocketknife is coming to a close.

It's not all right dying. Proceeding
from my left hand: paper leaves,

a paper doll cut, a tension left desire.
Is it right? Lighting up a vain

mirror, right, mirror, sanity left. Period.
I had to learn to lose my money, to gain trust, to brain disfavor,

to lead the right cheer, not to be unseemly.
I keep my left pant leg on. Random Fashion

and take some trust from a paper dollar nation.
Maybe when I left them I was not right

but a human has a right to try her human feeling
then take the ship that's left and steer it through its reeling.

"A STORY ABOUT OVERCOMING HARDSHIP TOLD BY A FRIEND"

Lolita with the glasses
as told by the glasses

because she would not change
her name and so the objects
around her changed her name –

or face –

by which I mean, the associations speak –

part one: flapping hands –
we are not mouthing ohs, ah-ahs,
ha!

it depends on the color of the airplane –

this is me – the glasses commenting
you could say annoyed –

the shadow was the Humberts
in front and she was just alive

light, kind of irritating
but where are we without it –

hitting the dark with sticks
or crawling towards

intensity – a heavy edge
falls on skin: on screen!

and now the other –

consider the heart in glasses a tension headache –

you press a bottle and it breaks
you are underwater because knowing
you go into the holes with bottles
and break them. I am underwater
because I would go into the holes with
a bottle – I would be in a bottle –
I was a bottle who was underwater in a bottle
I was underwater – I saw a hole
it was a bottle – I was
underwater meaning I was mostly asleep
I was asleep and I thought I should ask him
to take a picture of me asleep because
I wanted to see who that was –

it was a bottle – did you see it too?

you were looking for the Lolita twins –
they were your neighbors when you lived in
California but then it was only
this one girl   who was nice to you –

before you were a boy you were a dog –

she'd achieved the questionable distinction
of being buried alive –

and came back a wolf – radiant the threats
about your head – no one
particular canister, you find a life

inside a life: the crickets at night –

when I mention the rope around the neck
as well as the separation
you come to see the –

full blown tether –
the girl in the neighboring yard seeing
you – what comes at you as different –

it occurs to me that the ego decay you'd
been experiencing is a sense of confusion

existentially that – the edge of yourself has so many
empty spaces that (can) and do –
       with
and then there was the one person extending to exist
in an edge area –

like you, I cannot bark forever –

you've become essential to many people.

up went three canisters, one returns –

it was a strange way to split – to mingle with the mind
form one chasing another preceding
a species of the rods and cones

like light and no words –
underwater emulsion develops the figures

among their poisonous chemicals

on the frequency line – proportional to the letter
say, Times New Roman,

north –
  south, south, east –
north –

  that story's heard song is over—

on new land the space we made
in case someone actually

  us or   kind of   like us

  at any rate we're safe

and this is I mean I am
like you   alive

IN THE BEGINNING

First wind that is me.
You are gold so I

am your ore. Until

I am water. You
are fish and river.

I become one-eyed
beware. You're aware.

A bellows blowing.

I am an inkhorn.
You are an inkhorn.

I am uncertain.
You – leather bottle

whereas I am flask.
You are uncertain.

I am web and loom.
You are a lamb suit.

I, Cynewulf, eat you.

You become a key.

I am a keyhole.

You are copper beech.
I'm paper off that

tree. You are the lost

inkhorn. I see now.
I am a new book.

You sing and wander
so I am the moon.

You are a quill pen
drawing in a room

while I am light stone.

Or you are the Soul
and I am your soul.

CARBON

I am not your grandmother
but I could see why you'd think I was.
The soft teeth and uneasiness with traffic.
Children do this too. Uneasiness.

A toddler may throw a tantrum if the caregiver
feeds her with the wrong hand, for instance.
      Toddlers are grandmothers.
That is very obvious –

like they've just come from the construction
phase into our present consensus reality.
They are pissed by economics:
      the sugar visible everywhere –

      Give it here!
Counterman where ya going?
A star heavier than our present sun
produced these things we want.

The heavier star is everybody's grandmother
who is faster in the center, hotter in the center.
She makes finer things high up but her vibration
      may annoy us. Phasing like a headache.

Here, I've made my wagon.
Old cardboard.
 I take the long way
      science be damned.

Still, paper's real enough.
Eight pressed pages, the:
words enough for my present purposes.
Eaten and reformed, eaten and reformed.

Before the cardboard phase
agitations what's-his-name
                saying like a planet,
and that grandfather had it with us,

                I'd had it with the grandfather
and his degenerate singe-ers.
In an attic apartment with him, like I said
when I fell. Never said boo. Just nuts.

Now I'm fresh out of bubblegum.
                I refuse their castoffs, e.g.
the glamorized past, the vague now,
the future fouled by fear. I've come

crazy to conduct a color image
                or maybe very many.
And the friends I still have,
                I still want to have.

                Human's unite the Quantum
world with the world of classical physics
with theirs senses
and their languages urge.

In my Grandmother's clutch
or handbag you can get it if it can be gotten
and it works better if it's gotten for all.
FYI a present world, IMO reachable.

THIS NOW

ONE

When I went through your door this morning
I wore the old black eyes of early wurm.

By wurm I mean world embryo or frog since it's round
and will make sound soon sometime (my faith it is to say).

A circle seeks a circle. Is that weird? Incorrect?

Say in my ear a straight line so I can declare "I".
Lend me a pin to point to my base to drive it home.

By base I mean feet, by feet I mean what I've done
well. What I think I've done well. Subjectively well done.

There are six basic spokes from my center, you have more.

Wheels turn by hand and feet and throat and mind from the heat
of the head. That I died last night: yes. That I'm alive

is more true now. A hermaphrodite. You know this well
accept it as though, as me you would love to be too.

For inevitable noise, I've made alternate lines.

I love this good trick, I love this trick love, being switched
with you. It seems we are very different at times too.

We sleep where we are and where we think we are: the sound
of sounds are different from each other logically.

TWO

To wake and know the cabinets incredible
know where the cabinet food goes and its many tastes.

I rummage through the cabinets of this place sleeping
and all your eyes line up on the floor as staying words.

I like because it's good. Its good to like. I don't care.

Or I wake in the memory of money: old rope.
A wild germ feeds my rope idea. That's how I choke.

Plane acid spoils a sector of memories: close now.
Behind one door: seeds in a jar below empty jars.

Outer air can't enter this fermentation process.

From the cabinet in the cabinet you go out.
There are tricks to teach the sailing ships— their memories.

I do not want memories but I want to know things.
I don't care. Love is logic and invisibly on

among other things. The problem of desirous rings.

They yell feeding time being teeth and stomach's stomach.
Growing nails and hair inside, in another stomach.

In another swelling a stomach, in another
stomach a swelling. Do not let this thing swallow you

I'm saying this to me and you. I want to be done

with the old, old radioactive material.
I say to you: think this river. That is me, to cross.

When you go through me I am able to go through you.
The knowing holding, the knowing holding, holding us.

Where was I? Is to know to go there? Do you care?
Life's response is I was going to say how nothing takes it away

but no it is like everywhere, right? And from the inside you
meet people we once were and now stand next to.

ACKNOWLEDGMENTS

Thank you! Everyone, but especially Josh Edwards, Nick Twemlow, Lynn Xu and Robyn Schiff at Canarium Books for publishing my poems, and the editors of:

Fence Magazine, who first published "Inverse Heaven Division One," "Inverse Heaven Division Two," and "Eggheads and Rejects in and around Science Fiction Society"

Lungfull! Magazine, who first published "Philadelphia Alternate Science Fiction Society News"

Notnostrums who first published "From a Book of Changes," and *blog.bestamericanpoetry.com*, where it appeared again

Coldfront for first publishing "This Is Also a Dolphin"

jubilat for first publishing "On a Level"

Triple Canopy for first publishing "Like on the Subject of . . ."

The Academy of American Poets for publishing "Bows from the Last Dance" on their website: www.poets.org

Versal Magazine for publishing "R 1," "R 2," "R 3," and "R 5"

Boog City Reader 8 for publishing "Miss Is Not" (as "Miss Is Not Just a Plucky Fork")

LiVE Mag for first publishing "Circular Runes"

The Sonnets: Translating and Rewriting Shakespeare for publishing "Gole 83"

Anomalous Press for first publishing "Bridge Rhapsody"

OnandOnscreen for first publishing "Line of Reality"

Epiphany Magazine for first publishing "In the Beginning"

Poor Claudia for publishing "Carbon" in their online journal, *Crush 8*

Everyday Genius for first publishing "This Now"

Incessant Pipe for first publishing "A Story about Overcoming . . ."

Thank you to the people at the Helen Zell Writers' Program at the University of Michigan for sponsoring Canarium Books.

Also thank you to the following people for their kind inclusiveness: Rebecca Wolf, Rob Arnold, Clay Banes, Shannon Burns, Jackie Clark, Buck Downs, Jess Puglisi, Brendan Lorber, Alex Dimitrov, Brian Foley, Jennifer Nelson, Lucy Ives, Thomas Devaney, David Kirschenbaum, Jeffrey Ciphers Wright, Paul Legault, Sharmila Cohen, Heather Christle, Emily Petit, Guy Petit, Robert Fernandez, Megan Garr, Shannon C. Walsh, Jeffrey Pethybridge, Peter Gizzi, Lydia Wilson, Dara Wier, Mary Hickman, Drew Scott Swenhaugen, Marshall Walker Lee and Rae Armantrout.

Love to the people of CRVPT: Stella Corso, Wilson Yerxa, Casey Shanahan, John Sieracki, David Fienstein, David Pritchard, Amanda Robinson, Sarah Beth Mcalpine, Andy McAlpine, Jonathan Volk and our friends Gabe, Ariana, Karl, Gretchen, Jed and Emily. And gamers Bob, Chris and Kiri.

I am grateful that you exist and that we can share time on earth.

Thanks family: Val, Jim, Heather and Lily; hope you like the book.

Finally Greg C. Purcell (see pages 85 & 86).

Ish Klein is the author of *UNION!*, *Moving Day* and *Consolation and Mirth*, all published by Canarium Books. She is a founding member of the Connecticut River Valley Poets Theater (CRVPT) wherein she writes plays, including: *Drummer 41* and the Faust remake: *In A Word, Faust*. A DVD compilations of her videos, *Success Window*, was released by Poor Claudia. She lives in Amherst, Massachusetts with her partner: writer Greg C. Purcell.